THIS TEXTBOOK BELONGS TO

....

....

....

....

Hebrew 3 Textbook: Learn to Read Hebrew Using the Nikud Vowel System and Letters – for Teens and Adults – Soft Cover B&W Interior

2nd Edition

© 2021 Hebrew by Inbal™ LLC
All Rights Reserved.

ISBN: 979-8-9921693-3-1

LCCN: 2025901012

UNLOCK THE FINAL STEP
IN READING & WRITING

Holy Hebrew, you've already done an incredible job completing Hebrew 1 & 2! You've mastered the Print and Cursive Script alphabets, nailing all your writing skills in Hebrew. Now, you're ready to conquer all your reading skills by unlocking the essential tool of the Hebrew language: the Nikud vowel system. This textbook (and yours truly) have your back, guiding you to confidently read and write Hebrew with Nikud.

YOUR HEBREW TRAINING WHEELS

The Nikud vowel system acts like trusty training wheels as you begin your Hebrew reading and writing journey, helping you read any word with ease. Over time, you'll find yourself relying on it less as your vocabulary grows. But even seasoned Hebrew speakers and native pros rely on Nikud to distinguish between words that share spelling but have different meanings, dive into biblical texts, and explore Hebrew literature.

DESIGNED FOR YOUR SUCCESS

This textbook is the result of careful simplification and months of creative work. Say goodbye to unnecessary frustration and hello to a practical, streamlined approach to Hebrew. By the end of this textbook and its extensive practice, you'll be ready to start reading any Hebrew text you come across using the Nikud vowel system!

JOIN THE FREE COURSE FOR SUPER SMOOTH SAILING!

This textbook comes with a free course where I guide you every step of the way. Enroll now at **learn.hebrewbyinbal.com/1447** to access:

- My step-by-step walkthrough of the textbook
- Feedback on the extensive practice exercises included in this book
- Your direct line of VIP support — ask me any question!
- My proprietary phonetic system used in this book and in all my programs

Don't miss out on this valuable resource — enroll in the free course before starting the textbook to make your learning journey super smooth!

See you there!

Lesson 1:

USING YOUR WRITING SKILLS IN HEBREW TO COMPLETE YOUR READING SKILLS

YOU KNOW ALL THE LETTERS AND HOW TO WRITE. NOW, HOW DO YOU READ?

Hooray! You started this textbook which means you've got the entire Hebrew alphabet under your belt (way to go, you!).

That also means that you know

THE LETTER BET בּ MAKES A /B/ SOUND LIKE IN BANANA

In this textbook, we're going to add to your knowledge the Hebrew Vowel system called Nikud /nee-'kood/ נִיקוּד in Hebrew

בננה

This is how you write "Banana" in Hebrew (without Nikud)

YOU KNOW ALL THE LETTERS AND HOW TO WRITE. NOW, HOW DO YOU READ?

The SOUND that you learned each Hebrew letter makes is its CONSONANT sound.

THE LETTER BET בּ MAKES A CONSONANT /B/ SOUND

By learning how to read the Nikud signs around the letters, and the vowel sounds in Hebrew, you'll be able to read and write every word in Hebrew!

בָּנָנָה

These Nikud signs around the letters tell us how to read them

Lesson 2:

CONSONANTS & VOWELS

THE TWO SOUNDS OF SPOKEN LANGUAGES

The most basic unit of any spoken language is known as a SOUND (or UTTERANCE, if we're feeling extra brainy).

Spoken languages have two main types of SOUND:

CONSONANTS

Produced by keeping your mouth relatively closed, with little to no air flow

VOWELS

Produced by opening your mouth wider, creating more air flow

CONSONANT SOUNDS IN ENGLISH

Let's look at CONSONANT SOUNDS in English

All letters in English can function as consonants, Vowel letters can function as consonants or vowels. As a consonant, each letter makes its dedicated sound. Practice it by vocalizing the sound made by each circled letter in these English words, as if it were standalone and not part of the word:

A(P)(P)LE

(I)R(I)S

(B)A(N)A(N)A

(C)A(M)E(L)

(L)E(G)

(U)(N)(D)E(R)

These are consonant sounds!

VOWEL SOUNDS IN ENGLISH

Now let's look at vowel sounds in English.

The letters (A E I O U Y) can function as vowels or as consonants. As vowels, they either produce no sound (are silent) or a sound that combines their vowel sound and the consonant sound of the letter before them, creating a syllable. Practice it by vocalizing the sound produced by the circled letter(s) only in these English words:

APPL(E)

IRI(S)

(B)A(N)A(N)A

C(A)MEL

L(E)G

UN(DE)R

These are vowel sounds!

CONSONANT & VOWEL SOUNDS ENGLISH VS. HEBREW

Now, let's meet the similarities and differences between the English and Hebrew vowel systems.

Just Like in English

Every letter in Hebrew acts as a consonant. The four Hebrew vowel letters can act as consonants or vowels. As vowels, they make no sound, or a sound combining their vowel sound and the consonant sound of the letter before them.

Unlike in English

Hebrew has signs called Nikud, which are small lines and dots around the letters. These signs guide us how to pronounce the letters, and whether one of the four vowel letters acts as a vowel or as a consonant.

Lesson 3:

THE PHONETIC GAME-CHANGER SYSTEM

THE PSP: YOUR BRIDGE FROM WRITING TO SPEAKING HEBREW

Welcome to the lesson that will revolutionize your Hebrew language learning experience!

Whether you've completed Hebrew 1 and/or 2 workbooks, or are new to my PSP (Phonetic System for Pronunciation), this lesson is for you!

If you're already familiar with the PSP, this lesson serves as an important refresh to ensure that you're able to master the Hebrew vowel system and read every word in this textbook perfectly.

If you're new to the PSP, don't worry. In this lesson, I will show you how to use my exclusive system to read and pronounce every Hebrew sound and word simply and perfectly.

I'll teach you how to harness the power of the PSP to simplify the Hebrew vowel system and learn the long list of words in this textbook with ease.

With the PSP, you'll be able to read and pronounce Hebrew words just like a native speaker. And the best part? You'll be able to apply these skills beyond this textbook across all my lessons and programs.

From consonants to vowels, and everything in between, this lesson will equip you with the knowledge you need to bridge from reading to speaking Hebrew like a pro.

So, whether you're a seasoned pro or new to my Phonetic System for Pronunciation (PSP), get ready to unlock the power of the Hebrew language with my tried-and-true system!

YOUR KEY TO SUCCESS: THE PSP TABLE & VIDEOS

On page 17, you'll find the PSP table, your essential tool for pronouncing Hebrew words and sounds like a native. Here's a quick sample of each sound presented in the table:

When you see this letter

Acts as a consonant

Acts as a vowel

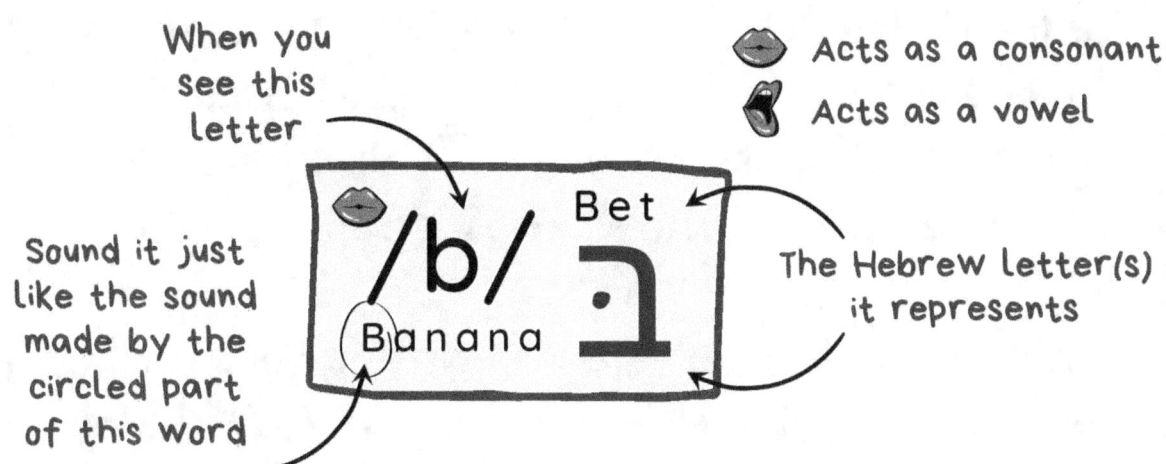

Sound it just like the sound made by the circled part of this word

/b/

Bet

ב

Banana

The Hebrew letter(s) it represents

If you haven't already, this is a friendly reminder to use the free course that comes with this textbook. Enroll for free at learn.hebrewbyinbal.com/1447
Inside the course, I guide you through the PSP and more in videos to make your learning super smooth, fun, and easy.

PSP TABLE:
IMPORTANT POINTS

A few important points regarding the PSP Table:

First, letters Alef א and Ayeen ע are not in the table because they make an /a/, /e/, /ee/, /o/ or /oo/ sound based on their vowel/Nikud.

Second, the letter names are presented in the table as they are read based on the PSP. In some cases, this spelling differs from how they're formally written.

Third, the letter He ה can make a soft /h/ sound following an /a/ or /e/ vowel at the end of a word, which is written using the PSP as /ah/ or /eh/.

And finally, the table is divided into consonant sounds and vowel sounds. Under the vowel sounds, you won't find any Hebrew letters assigned. You will learn the Hebrew vowel letters and the Nikud signs used for each of these vowel sounds in this textbook.

CONSONANTS

/b/ **ב** Bet — Banana	/g/ **ג** Geemel — Guitar	/d/ **ד** Dalet — Door	/h/ **ה** He — Hand
/v/ **ב ו** Vav Vet — Vet	/z/ **ז** Zayeen — Zoo	/kh/ **כ ח** Khet Khaf — Khalah	
/t/ **ת ט** Tet Tav — Ten	/y/ **י** Yod — Yes	/k/ **ק כּ** Kaf Kof — Keep	
/l/ **ל** Lamed — Leg	/m/ **מ** Mem — Moon	/n/ **נ** Noon — No	
/s/ **שׂ ס** Samekh Seen — Sand	/p/ **פּ** Pe — Pen	/f/ **פ** Fe — Flower	
/ts/ **צ** Tsadee — Pizza	/r/ **ר** Resh — Rain	/sh/ **שׁ** Sheen — Shake	

VOWELS

/a/ Father   /e/ Pet   /ee/ Beep   /o/ Or   /oo/ Oops

READ HEBREW WORDS PERFECTLY LIKE A NATIVE IN ENGLISH USING THE PSP

In this book, you'll meet Hebrew words presented to you in English, in Hebrew, and in English letters using the PSP. Whenever you see English letters between two forward slashes /like this/, that means it's a Hebrew word written using the PSP. This is how it looks for letter names:

/bet/

ב

/vav/

ו

/yod/

י

To help you break down each word, I separate the syllables using a - dash sign between them, like this:

/gee-mel/

ג

/da-let/

ד

/za-yeen/

ז

In addition, I indicate which syllable is stressed in each word.
This way, you can read and pronounce every word in Hebrew perfectly, like a native speaker.

When writing the word in English using the PSP, I use the apostrophe ' sign at the beginning of the syllable stressed in that word.

In this textbook only, when writing the word in Hebrew, I use the < sign above the syllable stressed in that word.

This is how it looks like (adding Nikud signs to the Hebrew writing as we learn each one):

Morning   /'bo-ker/   בֹּקֶר

Cowboy   /bo-'ker/   בֹּקֶר

Lesson 4:

THE NIKUD SIGNS

THE NIKUD LINES & DOTS

The Nikud /nee-'kood/ נִיקוּד system is a set of small lines and dots added around the Hebrew letters to indicate their sound / pronunciation.

The word 'Nikud' comes from the Hebrew word /ne-koo-'dot/ נְקוּדוֹת which means Dots in Hebrew. Understanding the Nikud system is essential for reading and writing in Hebrew, whether you are a beginner or an advanced reader. In the following lessons, we'll dive into the five vowel sounds in Hebrew represented by the Nikud signs:

/a/   /e/   /ee/   /o/   /oo/

The Nikud system is considered a daunting topic by many, especially since each of the five vowel sounds has multiple Nikud signs representing different lengths of sound. But fear not! This textbook is unique in its simplifying approach, helping you master everything you need to use the Nikud system, and read Hebrew like any Israeli as you complete this book.

YOU'RE OFFICIALLY READY TO DIVE INTO THE FIVE HEBREW VOWEL SOUNDS:

/a/

Pronounced like the letter A in the word FATHER

/e/

Pronounced like the letter E in the word PET

/ee/

Pronounced like the letters EE in the word BEEP

/o/

Pronounced like the letter O in the word OR

/oo/

Pronounced like the letters OO in the word OOPS

Lesson 5:

/A/
VOWEL SOUND

The
/a/
vowel sound
is pronounced
like the
letter a
in the word Father

LET'S SIMPLIFY
LEARNING THE /A/ NIKUD SIGNS:

We'll focus on the two commonly used Nikud signs for the /a/ vowel sound out of the total four that exist.

You can find and learn all Nikud signs, including the less common ones, on page 125.

On the next pages, you'll learn the two common Nikud signs for the /a/ vowel sound.
It's important to know the sound both represent.
You can use either sign of the two when writing, as the differences are so subtle that even most native Hebrew speakers wouldn't know the formal one of the two for a specific word.
As your Hebrew teacher, I always show you the formal Nikud signs for each word.

THE FIRST NIKUD SIGN FOR /A/ VOWEL SOUND LOOKS LIKE THIS (X REPRESENTS THE LETTER)

This Nikud sign is under the letter.

To write this Nikud sign, draw a horizontal line from left to right, and then a straight line in the middle going down (there is no need to make the line thicker at the bottom). Always follow the specific order and direction when drawing Nikud signs, just like with writing Hebrew letters.

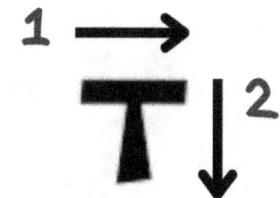

EASILY REMEMBER THIS NIKUD SIGN AND THE SOUND IT MAKES

This Nikud sign

ㅜ

looks like a tie

The **/a/** vowel sound is pronounced like the letter A in the word Father

This Nikud sign that looks like a FATHER'S TIE makes an /a/ sound like the /a/ in the word FATHER.

LET'S USE THIS NIKUD SIGN TO READ HEBREW WORDS

סַל

A Basket in Hebrew is /sal/

When reading Hebrew, we start with the rightmost letter and move left.
For each letter, we identify its consonant sound, and then check the Nikud sign to determine the vowel sound.
We repeat this for each letter until we reach the last letter on the left.

The first letter is Samekh, which makes a consonant /s/ sound. Combined with the /a/ Nikud sign, the first letter is read as /sa/.

The second letter is Lamed, which makes a consonant /l/ sound. Being the last letter with no Nikud sign, it is read as a consonant /l/.

READ EACH NEW WORD ALOUD TO ENSURE YOU UNDERSTAND ITS SPELLING AND SOUND:

מָרָק

Soup in Hebrew is /ma-'rak/

The < sign in Hebrew, and the ' sign in English are my way of showing you what syllable to stress in multi-syllable words. They are not part of the Hebrew writing.

The first letter is Mem, which makes a consonant /m/ sound. Combined with the /a/ Nikud sign, it is read as /ma/

The second letter is Resh, which makes a consonant /r/ sound. Combined with the /a/ Nikud sign, it is read as /ra/

The last letter is Kof (also spelled Qof), which makes a consonant /k/ sound. Being the last letter with no Nikud sign, it's read as a consonant /k/

THE SECOND NIKUD SIGN FOR /A/ VOWEL SOUND LOOKS LIKE THIS (X REPRESENTS THE LETTER)

This Nikud sign is under the letter.

To draw this Nikud sign, draw a horizontal line from left to right, just like the first Nikud sign you learned, and stop there. As with Hebrew letters, always follow the specific order and direction when writing Nikud signs.

1 →

‗

EASILY REMEMBER THIS NIKUD SIGN AND THE SOUND IT MAKES

This Nikud sign

—

looks like a father's tie with its bottom part cut off

The /a/ vowel sound is pronounced like the letter A in the word Father

The Nikud sign that looks like a FATHER'S TIE with the bottom part cut off makes an /a/ sound like the /a/ in the word FATHER

READ THIS BRRR... WORD:

קַר

> Cold (referring to temperature or weather) in its default/masculine form is is /kar/

* In Hebrew, adjectives usually have both masculine and feminine forms.

Kof (also spelled Qof) is the first letter. It makes a consonant /k/ sound. Combined with the /a/ Nikud sign, it is read as /ka/.	The second letter is Resh, which makes a consonant /r/ sound. Being the last letter with no Nikud sign, it is read as a consonant /r/.

GET YOUR HEBREW FLOWING:

נַחַל

A stream in Hebrew is /'na-khal/

* The < sign in Hebrew, and the ' sign in English are my way of showing you what syllable to stress in multi-syllable words for a correct and local pronunciation..
They are not part of the Hebrew writing.

The first letter is Nun /noon/, which makes a consonant /n/ sound. Combined with the /a/ Nikud sign, it is read as /na/.

The second letter is Khet, which makes a consonant /kh/ sound. Combined with the /a/ Nikud sign, it is read as /kha/.

The last letter is Lamed, which makes a consonant /l/ sound. Being the last letter with no Nikud sign, we read it as a consonant, making a consonant /l/ sound.

READY TO READ WORDS WITH BOTH /A/ NIKUD SIGNS?

** I always present the formal Nikud sign for each letter and word. You can use either of the two /a/ Nikud signs interchangeably when writing.

טַבָּח

A cook/chef in Hebrew in its default/masculine form is /ta-'bakh/

The first letter is Tet, which makes a consonant /t/ sound. Combined with the /a/ Nikud sign, it is read as /ta/.

The second letter is Bet with a Dugesh, which makes a consonant /b/ sound. Combined with the /a/ Nikud sign, it is read as /ba/.

Moving on to the last letter, we have Khet, which makes a consonant /kh/ sound. Being the last letter with no Nikud sign, we read it as a consonant /kh/ sound.

WHAT DO WE CALL THESE NIKUD SIGNS?

Learning the names of the Nikud signs is optional, as it's not essential for reading or writing Hebrew perfectly using Nikud.

If you want to know the names of the Nikud signs, here's an easy tip for you:
The first syllable of each Nikud sign name matches the vowel sound of that Nikud sign.
This rule applies to all Nikud signs.

קָמָץ

This Nikud sign is called /ka-ˈmats/

פַתָח

This Nikud sign is called /pa-ˈtakh/

The first syllable of Kamats and Patakh is /a/ matching the vowel sound they represent: /a/

/A/ VOWEL SOUND: SUMMARY

The **/a/** vowel sound is pronounced like the letter A in the word Father

There are two commonly used Nikud signs that represent the /a/ vowel sound. You can use either of the two interchangeably, knowing that both represent basically the same sound:

ָ

‐

/ka-'mats/

/pa-'takh/

קָמֵץ

פַּתֵח

To remember these two common Nikud signs for /a/, think of a father's tie, with or without the bottom part

We draw it from left to right, (and top to bottom in the case of the Kamats), under the letter

PRACTICE YOUR WAY TO MASTERING READING

The best way to get comfortable with the Hebrew vowel system is by practicing — just like learning to write!
This textbook gives you all you need to do that, with extensive practice exercises at the end of each lesson. Make sure to use them so everything you learn really sticks. And if you have the Hebrew 1 and/or 2 Workbooks, we'll use them for extra practice!

In the practice exercises, I'll show you the formal Nikud for each word, and when there's more than one option (like with the /a/ vowel sound), I'll include all the alternatives you can use interchangeably. These exercises are an invaluable tool to sharpen your skills with the Hebrew vowel system — take full advantage of them.

LET'S PRACTICE!
The /a/ Vowel Sound

ADD NIKUD SIGNS TO THE WORDS BELOW

If you have Hebrew 1 or 2 Workbooks or my
Hebrew Notebooks, use them for practice.
If not, grab a lined notebook — and if possible,
turn it to be right-to-left!

WAVE	SNAKE	SALAD
גל	נחֹשׁ	סלט
/gal/	/na-'khash/	/sa-'lat/

ONION	MOUNTAIN	CAMEL
בצל	הר	גמל
/ba-'tsal/	/har/	/ga-'mal/

If you have Hebrew 1 Workbook,
add Nikud to the words on pages 20, 31, 86.

If you have Hebrew 2 Workbook,
add Nikud to the words on pages 16, 31, 86.

Check how you did inside the free course.

Lesson 6:

THE STOP
NIKUD SIGN

THE NIKUD SIGN THAT STOPS TRAFFIC

In this lesson, you'll learn about a unique Nikud sign that ensures a letter is read as a consonant rather than a vowel. While most Nikud signs indicate a vowel sound, this one tells us the letter should be pronounced as a consonant with no vowel sound.

You've already learned that when the last letter of a word has no Nikud, it's read as a consonant.
Now, we're adding another case: when this Nikud sign appears, it either stops the vowel sound or holds it in place.

This Nikud sign can also indicate an /e/ sound. We'll see exactly when that happens in Lesson 7, dedicated to the /e/ vowel sound.

THE CONSONANT NIKUD SIGN LOOKS LIKE THIS (X REPRESENTS THE LETTER)

This Nikud sign is under the letter.

Draw it by making 2 dots one on top of the other, starting with the top one.

Just like with Hebrew letters, it is important to follow the specific order and direction when drawing the Nikud signs.

1

2

EASILY REMEMBER THIS NIKUD SIGN AND THE SOUND IT MAKES

This Nikud sign

looks like two lights in a traffic light.

Just like the red and yellow (not flashing) lights in a traffic light — it signals to stop or prepare to stop = consonant sound.

LET'S USE THIS NIKUD SIGN TO READ HEBREW WORDS:

Read about the dot inside the Dalet letter on p. 124

סַנְדָּ֫ל

A sandal in Hebrew is /san-'dal/

The first letter is Samekh, which makes a consonant /s/ sound. Combined with the /a/ Nikud sign, it is read as /sa/.

The second letter is Nun, making a consonant /n/ sound. Combined with the Stop Nikud sign, it is read as a consonant /n/.

the third letter is Dalet, which makes a consonant /d/ sound. Combined with the /a/ Nikud sign, it is read as /da/.

The last letter is Lamed, which makes a consonant /l/ sound. Being the last letter with no Nikud sign, we read it as a consonant /l/.

SPIN THIS ONE LIKE A PRO:

Read about the dot inside the Gimel letters on p. 124

גַּלְגַּל

Read about the dot inside the Gimel letters on p. 124

A wheel in Hebrew is /gal-'gal/

The first letter is Gimel, which makes a consonant /g/ sound. Having an /a/ Nikud sign, it is read as /ga/.

The second letter is Lamed, making a consonant /l/ sound. It has a stop Nikud sign, so it is read as a consonant /l/.

the third letter is Gimel, which makes a consonant /g/ sound. Having an /a/ Nikud sign, it is read as /ga/.

The last letter is Lamed, which makes a consonant /l/ sound. Being the last letter with no Nikud sign, it is read as a consonant /l/.

LET'S READ THIS NIKUD SIGN AT THE BEGINNING OF A WORD

כְּתָב

The noun 'Writing' in Hebrew is /k-'tav/

The first letter is Kaf (with a Dugesh), which makes a consonant /k/ sound. It has a stop / consonant Nikud sign, so we read it as a consonant /k/.

the second letter is Tav, which makes a consonant /t/ sound. Having an /a/ Nikud sign, it is read as /ta/.

The last letter is Bet with no Dugesh, which makes a consonant /v/ sound. Being at the end of the word with no Nikud sign, we read it as a consonant /v/.

WHAT DO WE CALL THIS NIKUD SIGN?

You already know that learning the names of the Nikud signs is optional, and not essential for reading or writing Hebrew perfectly using Nikud.

If you'd like to learn the names of the Nikud signs, here's that easy tip again: The first syllable of each Nikud sign name matches the vowel sound of the Nikud sign. This rule applies to all Nikud signs.

שְׁוָא נָח

This Nikud sign is called /sh-'va nakh/

The first syllable in Shva is read as a consonant, just like the (consonant, no vowel) sound this Nikud sign represents.

STOP NIKUD SIGN: SUMMARY

The **STOP** Nikud sign stops a vowel/syllable sound in its place = is read as a consonant (no vowel sound).

It has a second use indicating an /e/ vowel sound. You'll learn exactly when that is the case in the next lesson.

:

/sh-'va nakh/

שׁוֹא נָח

Just like the top two lights of a traffic signal indicate 'stop', the two dots of a Shva symbolize a linguistic stop — no vowel sound.

We draw it by making two dots one on top of the other, from top to bottom, under the letter.

Lesson 7:

/E/
VOWEL SOUND

The **/e/** vowel sound is pronounced like the letter E in the word Pet

LET'S SIMPLIFY LEARNING THE /E/ NIKUD SIGNS:

We focus on the two commonly used Nikud signs for the /e/ vowel sound, out of the total four that exist.

To learn all about the two less common Nikud signs, go to page 125.

On the next pages, you'll learn the two common Nikud signs for the /e/ vowel sound.
It's important to know the sound both represent.
You can use either sign of the two when writing, as the differences between then are very subtle, and most native Hebrew speakers wouldn't know the formal one of the two for a specific word.
As your Hebrew teacher, I always show you the formal Nikud sign for each letter in a specific word.

THE FIRST NIKUD SIGN FOR /E/ VOWEL SOUND LOOKS LIKE THIS (X REPRESENTS THE LETTER)

This Nikud sign is under the letter.

To draw this Nikud sign, start with two dots side by side (starting with the left one), then add a third dot below, centered between them.

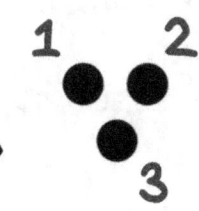

EASILY REMEMBER THIS NIKUD SIGN AND THE SOUND IT MAKES

This Nikud sign

looks like a dog's eyes and nose.

The **/e/** vowel sound is pronounced like the letter E in the word Pet

The Nikud sign - that looks like a dog's eyes and nose - makes an /e/ sound, like the letter E in the word Pet.

PAWSITIVELY WOOF-TASTIC:

כֶּ֫לֶב

Dog in Hebrew in its masculine form is /'ke-lev/

The first letter is Kaf with a Dugesh, which makes a consonant /k/ sound. Having an /e/ Nikud sign, it is read as /ke/.

The second letter is Lamed, which makes a consonant /l/ sound. Having an /e/ Nikud sign, it is read as /le/.

The last letter is Bet with no Dugesh, making a consonant /v/ sound. Being the last letter with no Nikud sign, it is read as a consonant /v/.

GET SOAKED IN HEBREW:

Read about the dot inside the letter Gimel on p. 124

גֶּשֶׁם

> Rain in Hebrew is /'ge-shem/

The first letter is Gimel, which makes a consonant /g/ sound. Having an /e/ Nikud sign, it is read as /ge/.

The second letter is Shin, making a consonant /sh/ sound. Having an /e/ Nikud sign, it is read as /she/.

The last letter is Mem (Sofit), which makes a consonant /m/ sound. Being the last letter with no Nikud sign, it is read as a consonant /m/.

THE SECOND NIKUD SIGN FOR /E/ VOWEL SOUND LOOKS LIKE THIS (X REPRESENTS THE LETTER)

This Nikud sign is under the letter.

To draw this Nikud sign, make two dots side by side starting with the left one (like the first /e/ Nikud sign you just learned), and stop there.

1   2

EASILY REMEMBER THIS NIKUD SIGN AND THE SOUND IT MAKES

This Nikud sign

• •

Looks like our dog's eyes.

The /e/ vowel sound is pronounced like the letter E in the word Pet

This Nikud sign - that looks like our dog's eyes - makes an /e/ sound, like the letter E in the word Pet.

LET'S LIGHT IT UP!

נֵר

A candle in Hebrew is /ner/

The first letter is Nun, which makes a consonant /n/ sound. Having an /e/ Nikud sign, it is read as /ne/.

The last letter is Resh, which makes a consonant /r/ sound. Being the last letter and having no Nikud sign, it is read as a consonant /r/.

חֵץ

An arrow in Hebrew is /khets/

LET'S READ WORDS WITH /A/ AND /E/ NIKUD SIGNS

חָבֵר

A friend in the generic / masculine form is /kha-'ver/

The first letter is Khet, which makes a consonant /kh/ sound. Having an /a/ Nikud sign, it is read as /kha/.

The second letter is Bet with no Dugesh, making a consonant /v/ sound. Having an /e/ Nikud sign, it is read as /ve/.

The last letter is Resh, which makes a consonant /r/ sound. Being the last letter with no Nikud sign, it's read as a consonant /r/.

WHAT DO WE CALL THESE NIKUD SIGNS?

As we said, learning the names of the Nikud signs is optional and not necessary to be able to read and write Hebrew using Nikud.

If you'd like to learn the names of the Nikud signs, here's that easy tip again:
The first syllable of each Nikud sign name matches the vowel sound of the Nikud sign.
This rule applies to all Nikud signs.

סֶגּוֹל

This Nikud sign is called /se-'gol/

צֵירֶה

This Nikud sign is called /tsey-'reh/

The first syllable of Tseyreh and Segol is
/e/
matching the vowel sound they represent:
/e/

/E/ VOWEL SOUND: SUMMARY

The **/e/** vowel sound is pronounced like the letter E in the word Pet

There are two commonly used Nikud signs that represent the /e/ vowel sound. You can use either of the two interchangeably, knowing that both represent basically the same sound:

/se-ˈgol/

סֶגּוֹל

We remember them as a dog's face: Two eyes, with or without the nose

•• /tsey-ˈreh/

צֵירֶה

We draw them from the top left going right (and then down in the case of the Segol), under the letter

LET'S PRACTICE
The /a/ and /e/ Vowel Sounds

ADD NIKUD SIGNS TO THE WORDS BELOW

If you have Hebrew 1 or 2 Workbooks or my
Hebrew Notebooks, use them for practice.
If not, grab a lined notebook — and if possible,
flip and use it right-to-left!

SUN	CARROT	MOVIE
שֶׁמֶשׁ	גֶּזֶר	סֶרֶט
/'she-mesh/	/'ge-zer/	/'se-ret/
FLOWER	BREAD	TIGER
פֶּרַח	לֶחֶם	נָמֵר
/'pe-rakh/	/'le-khem/	/na-'mer/

If you have Hebrew 1 Workbook,
add Nikud to the words on pages 40, 58.

If you have Hebrew 2 Workbook,
add Nikud to the words on pages 40, 48, 60.

Check how you did inside the free course.

THE STOP (SHVA) NIKUD SIGN ALSO REPRESENTS THE /E/ VOWEL SOUND

The name Shva refers to the Nikud sign that looks like two dots one on top of the other, positioned under the letter.
While Shva Nakh guides us to read a letter as a consonant (the stop sign you learned), there is another type of Shva: Shva Na.

Shva Na is drawn and positioned the same as the Shva Nakh, but the two represent different sounds: Shva Na guides us to read the letter with an /e/ vowel sound.

/e/ Sound ⠶ Consonant Sound
Stop sign

שׁוֹ נֵע
This Nikud sign is called /sh-'va na/

שׁוֹ נַח
This Nikud sign is called /sh-'va nakh/

WHEN TO READ SHVA AS A CONSONANT SOUND (AND NOT AS AN /E/ SOUND)

Hebrew doesn't make this one easy for us - it comes with a couple of rules we need to know. Let's break down the two main cases for reading the Shva sign as a stop sign.

CASE #1

At the end of a word

CASE #2

When the Shva appears at the end of a syllable = following a letter with a vowel sound.

LET'S SEE AN EXAMPLE OF CASES 1 AND 2

Read about the dot inside the second Tav letter on p. 124

The singular feminine past tense form of (you) 'wrote' is /ka-'tav-t/

The first letter is Kaf with a Dugesh making a consonant /k/ sound. It has an /a/ Nikud sign, and so it is read as /ka/. The second letter is Tav making a consonant /t/ sound. It has an /a/ Nikud sign, and so it is read as /ta/.

The third letter is Bet with no Dugesh making a consonant /v/ sound. It has a Shva sign, and since it appears at the end of a syllable, it acts as a Shva Nakh = making a consonant /v/ sound.

The last letter is Tav. Being at the end of the word, if it has a Shva sign (as in this case) or has no Nikud sign, that means it acts as a Shva Nakh, and we read it as a consonant /t/,

WHEN TO READ SHVA AS AN /E/ SOUND (AND NOT AS A CONSONANT)

As much as I love simplifying complex topics - which is what this textbook is all about - when it comes to knowing when to read the Shva as an /e/ sound, there's no way around learning a few more rules.

I do not want this to slow your progress. Keep the following rules handy so you can refer back to them as needed.

Don't feel like you need to memorize everything — especially if it disrupts your momentum or motivation, which matter far more at this stage of your journey.

Go over the rules, practice them, and keep moving forward.

WHEN TO READ SHVA AS AN /E/ SOUND

CASE #1

The first letter of the word has a Shva Nikud sign AND is Lamed, Mem, Nun, Resh, or Yod ל מ נ ר י

EXAMPLE OF CASE #1

A potato pancake or latke is /le-vee-'vah/

CASE #2

The first letter of the word has a Shva Nikud sign AND is followed by one of these letters: Alef, Khet, He, Ayin א ח ה ע

EXAMPLE OF CASE #2

Gates (gate in plural form) is /she-a-'reem/

WHEN TO READ SHVA AS AN /E/ SOUND

CASE #3

The first letter of the word has a Shva Nikud sign AND is one of these four formative letter prefixes:

/b/ בּ prefix used for: In, With, By
/k/ כּ prefix used for: As, Like
/l/ ל prefix used for: To, For
/v/ ו prefix used for: And

3 EXAMPLES OF CASE #3

וְיִשְׂרָאֵל֫   לְיִשְׂרָאֵל֫   בְּיִשְׂרָאֵל֫

"In Israel" in Hebrew is /be-yees-ra-'el/
"To Israel" in Hebrew is /le-yees-ra-'el/
"And Israel" in Hebrew is /ve-yees-ra-'el/

WHEN TO READ SHVA AS AN /E/ SOUND

CASE #4

The Shva is assigned to a letter mid-word AND is the first of two identical letters one next to each other

EXAMPLE OF CASE #4

Read about the dot inside the letter Gimel on p. 124

גּוֹרְרִים

The present plural masculine form (We, plural You, and They) of the Hebrew verb "Towing" is /go-re-'reem/.

WHEN TO READ SHVA AS AN /E/ SOUND

CASE #5

The Shva is assigned to a letter mid-word AND is the second of two Shva signs one after the other. The first Shva is read as a consonant (stop sign / Shva Nakh) at the end of a syllable, and the second Shva is read as an /e/ vowel sound (Shva Na).

EXAMPLE OF CASE #5

Read about the dot inside the letter Tav on p. 124

יִכְתְּבוּ

The masculine form of "They will write" in Hebrew is /yeekh-te-'voo/

I Hope You're Loving Your Textbook

Can I ask you to invest 60 seconds
in sharing your experience?
Your review is the most helpful
feedback for others looking for
good Hebrew resources, and
for me as the author.
Toda Rabah - thank you so much!

WHERE CAN I LEAVE A REVIEW?

Great question!
You can leave a review wherever you purchased the book,
or on **Amazon**, **Goodreads**, or **Google**.
See direct links inside the free course for this textbook.

Thank you so much again!

Lesson 8:

HEBREW VOWEL LETTERS

VOWEL SOUNDS ARE SET BY BOTH NIKUD SIGNS & VOWEL LETTERS

There are four letters in Hebrew that can be a consonant and a vowel.

Often used in Open Syllables (syllables that end with a vowel sound), these letters are usually silent:

י	ו	ה	א
Yod	Vav	He	Alef

PLUS The letters Vav and Yod can also be part of the Nikud signs as you'll see next (/ee/, /o/, /oo/)

FYI: The Vowel letters are commonly called /o-tee-'yot e-he-'vee/ אותיות אהו"י (their abbreviation, a/e - h - v - ee)

Let's start exploring the vowel letters:

THE LETTER ALEF AS A VOWEL IS SILENT
Commonly used after /a/ and /e/ vowels, but not only

אַבָּא

Father or Dad in Hebrew is /'a-ba/

The first letter is Alef. Alef can be both a consonant and a vowel. When Alef has a Nikud sign, it's a consonant, and its sound is based on its Nikud sign (in this case, it is /a/).

The second letter is Bet with a Dugest making a consonant /b/ sound. Having an /a/ Nikud sign, it is read as /ba/.

The last letter is Alef. Having no Nikud sign, it is a vowel. Alef as a vowel is silent, so it doesn't add any sound to the /ba/ sound we already mentioned.

THE LETTER HE AS A VOWEL IS SILENT
Commonly used after /a/ and /e/ vowels

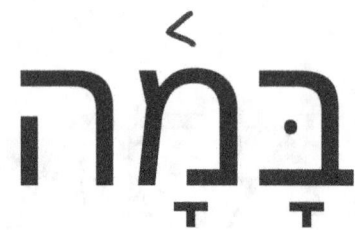

בָּמָה

A stage in Hebrew is /ba-'mah/

The first letter is Bet with a Dugesh. It makes a consonant /b/ sound. Having an /a/ Nikud sign, it is read as /ba/.

The second letter is Mem. It makes a consonant /m/ sound, and has an /a/ Nikud sign, therefore it's read as /ma/.

The last letter is He. Having no Nikud sign, it acts as a Vowel. Vowel He is silent with more air flow*: /mah/.

* Compared to Alef, the letter He as a Vowel involves more air flow (similar to the English H vs. the English A sound). We mark it using the PSP with the letter h at the end of a word.

QUICK REVIEW:
ALL YOU LEARNED SO FAR

/a/ and /e/ Vowel Sounds, The Stop (Shva) Nikud Sign, Alef & He Letters as Vowels

We start reading the letter at the far right of the word. First, we check the letter, and then its Nikud sign. We do the same with the Letter to its left, until we reach the last letter of the word:

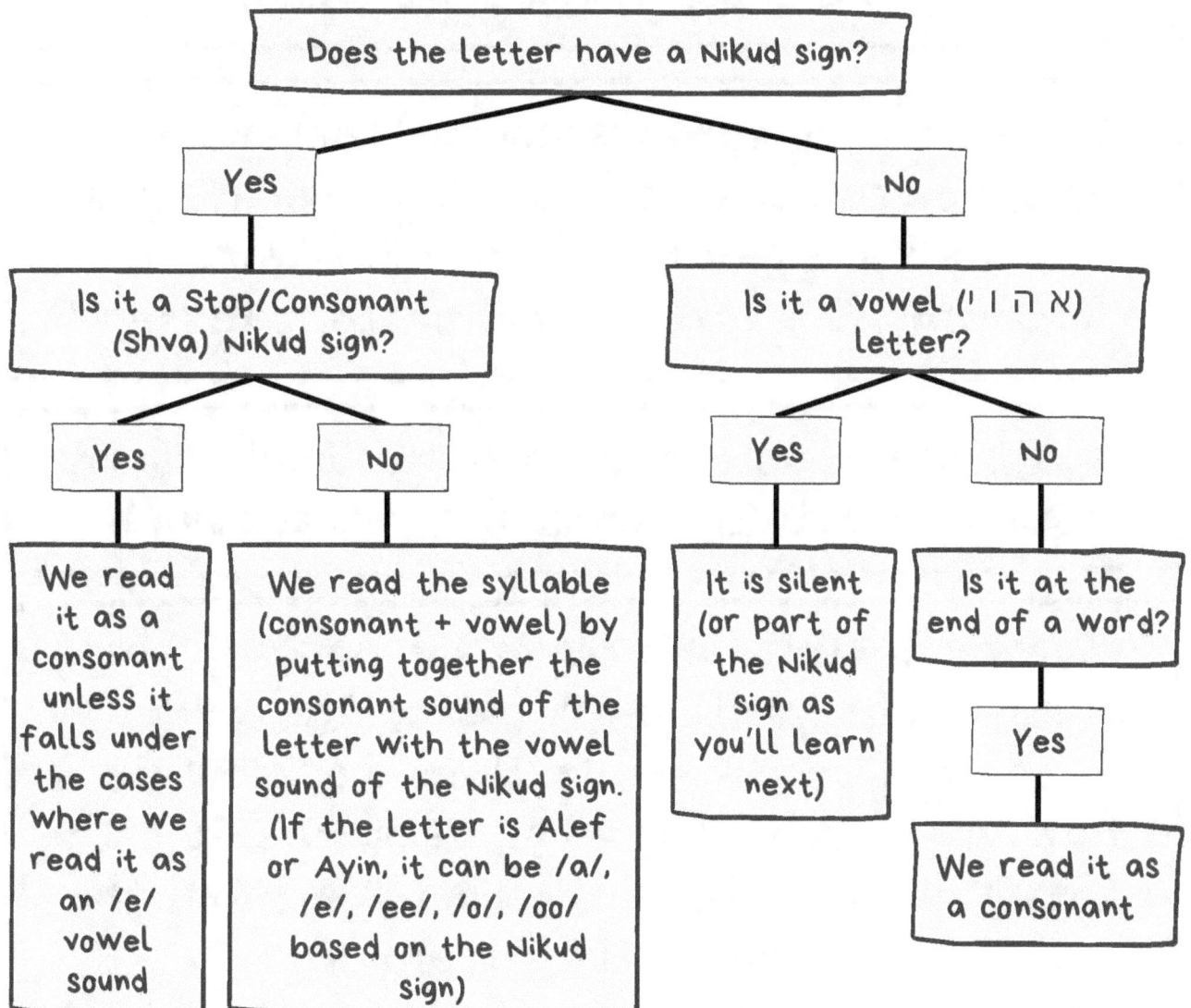

Does the letter have a Nikud sign?

Yes

No

Is it a Stop/Consonant (Shva) Nikud sign?

Is it a vowel (א ה ו י) letter?

Yes

No

Yes

No

We read it as a consonant unless it falls under the cases where we read it as an /e/ vowel sound

We read the syllable (consonant + vowel) by putting together the consonant sound of the letter with the vowel sound of the Nikud sign. (If the letter is Alef or Ayin, it can be /a/, /e/, /ee/, /o/, /oo/ based on the Nikud sign)

It is silent (or part of the Nikud sign as you'll learn next)

Is it at the end of a word?

Yes

We read it as a consonant

QUICK REVIEW:
ALL YOU LEARNED SO FAR

/a/ and /e/ Vowel Sounds, The Stop (Shva) Nikud
Sign, Alef & He Letters as Vowels

You can use the two common Nikud signs for /a/ and /e/ sounds interchangeably when writing using Nikud. When reading, know the sound these Nikud signs make.

If there is no vowel sound at the end of a word, you can skip using a Nikud sign. If there is a Nikud sign at the end of a word, it indicates the vowel sound of that letter.

A closed syllable ends in a consonant sound. An open syllable ends in a vowel sound.

Vowel letters are silent (or part of the Nikud sign, as you'll learn next). The vowel He at the end of a word involves more air flow than Vowel Alef (or Ayin). Using the PSP, the letter h marks both the consonant and the vowel He letter.

PUTTING IT INTO PRACTICE

ADD NIKUD SIGNS TO THE WORDS BELOW:

BUTTERFLY	**BOY**	**GRANDFATHER**
פרפר	ילד	סֹבא
/par-'par/	/'ye-led/	/'sa-ba/
FEMALE FRIEND or GIRLFRIEND	**GRANDMOTHER**	**QUEEN**
חברה	סֹבתא	מלכה
/kha-ve-'rah/	/'sav-ta/	/mal-'kah/

If you have Hebrew 1 Workbook,
add Nikud to the words on pages 10, 84.

If you have Hebrew 2 Workbook,
add Nikud to the words on pages 26, 28, 46.

Check how you did inside the free course.

PUTTING IT INTO PRACTICE

WRITE THE WORDS BELOW IN ENGLISH LETTERS USING THE PSP:

LETTUCE

חֲסָה

/ ? /

HARE

אַרְנָב

/ ? /

KING

מֶֽלֶךְ

/ ? /

BLESSING

בְּרָכָה

/ ? /

SNOW

שֶֽׁלֶג

/ ? /

LION

אַרְיֵה

/ ? /

Check how you did inside the free course.

Lesson 9:

/EE/
VOWEL SOUND

The
/ee/
vowel sound is
pronounced
like
the letters EE
in the word Beep

The /ee/ vowel sound in Hebrew can be represented by two different Nikud signs.

One includes the vowel Yod ׳ letter as part of it, and the other does not.

Let's start with the second option.

THE FIRST NIKUD SIGN FOR THE /EE/ VOWEL SOUND LOOKS LIKE THIS (X REPRESENTS THE LETTER):

This Nikud sign is under the letter.

Draw it by making one clear dot. Easy.

1

EASILY REMEMBER THIS NIKUD SIGN AND THE SOUND IT MAKES

This Nikud sign

●

looks like the beeping horn of a steering wheel

The /ee/ vowel sound is pronounced like the letters EE in the word BEEP

This Nikud sign that looks like the beeping horn of a steering wheel makes an /ee/ sound like the letters EE in the word BEEP.

THE MOTHER OF ALL WORDS:

Read about the dot inside the letter Mem on p. 124

אִמָּא

Mother in Hebrew is /'ee-ma/

| The first letter is Alef. It has a Nikud sign, therefore it is read as a consonant. Having an /ee/ Nikud sign, it is read as /ee/. | The second letter is Mem. Mem makes a consonant /m/ sound. Having an /a/ Nikud sign, it is read as /ma/. |

The last letter is Alef. It does not have a Nikud sign, therefore it is a vowel Alef, which is silent.

---

* The letter Alef א as a vowel is silent. As a consonant, it can make an /a/ /e/ /ee/ /o/ or /oo/ sound based on its Nikud sign. The letter Ayin ע is the same. That is why both are not included in the consonant letter section of the PSP table.

COZY UP:

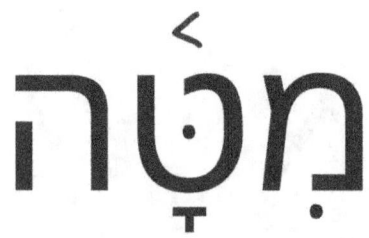

מִטָּה

Read about the dot inside the letter Tet on p. 124

A bed in Hebrew is /mee-'tah/

The first letter is Mem, which makes a consonant /m/ sound. Having an /ee/ Nikud sign, it's read as /mee/.

The second letter is Tet, which makes a consonant /t/ sound. Having an /a/ Nikud sign, it's read as /ta/.

The last letter is He. Having no Nikud sign means it is a vowel = is silent (with more air flow compared to Alef or Ayin, but the difference in sound is subtle).

Vowel He ה letter is silent. Compared to Vowel Alef א letter (which is also silent), Vowel He is pronounced with more air flow (like the English H vs. A letter), and is typically at the end of the word.

THE SECOND NIKUD SIGN FOR THE /EE/ VOWEL SOUND LOOKS LIKE THIS (X REPRESENTS THE LETTER)

This Nikud sign is under the letter, and has a Yod letter after it. The Yod letter has no Nikud sign, and is part of the /ee/ Nikud sign.

Draw it by making one dot (identical to the first Nikud sign for /ee/ you just learned), and following it will be a Yod ׳ letter

1

LET'S USE THIS NIKUD SIGN TO READ HEBREW WORDS:

פִּיל

An elephant in Hebrew is /peel/

The first letter is Pe, making a consonant /p/ sound. Having an /ee/ Nikud sign, it is read as /pee/.

The second letter is Yod. Yod can be a consonant or a vowel. This Yod has no Nikud sign and follows an /ee/ Nikud sign, which means it is part of the /ee/ Nikud sign.

The last letter is Lamed, which makes a consonant /l/ sound. Having no Nikud sign, it is read as a consonant /l/.

Vowel Yod is silent and is part of the /ee/ vowel sound and Nikud sign.

THE WEEKEND KICKOFF WORD

Read about the dot inside the letter Shin on p. 124

שִׁישִׁי

> Friday in Hebrew is /shee-'shee/

The first letter is Shin. Shin makes a consonant /sh/ sound. Having an /ee/ Nikud sign, it is read as /shee/.

The second letter is Shin. Shin makes a consonant /sh/ sound. Having an /ee/ Nikud sign, it is read as /shee/.

The last letter is Yod. Yod can be a consonant or a vowel. This Yod has no Nikud sign and follows an /ee/ Nikud sign, which means it is part of the /ee/ Nikud sign.

WHAT ARE THESE NIKUD SIGNS CALLED?

As you already know, the names of the Nikud signs are not needed for reading using Nikud. If you want to know the names of the Nikud signs, here's that easy tip again:
The first syllable of each Nikud sign name matches the vowel sound of the Nikud sign.
This rule applies to all Nikud signs.

Let's see how it works with the two /ee/ sound Nikud signs you just learned:

אִ   אִי

חִירִיק חָסֵר

This Nikud sign is called
/khee-'reek kha-'ser/

חִירִיק מָלֵא

This Nikud sign is called
/khee-'reek ma-'le/

The first syllable in /khee-'reek/ is /ee/ just like the sound it represents. The second words in each name refer to whether it has a Yod or not
(/ma-'le/ means Full= With a Yod, and /kha-'ser/ means Absent= Without a Yod).

REMEMBER: YOD י CAN ALSO BE A CONSONANT

שְׁמֵימִי

Heavenly is /sh-mey-'mee/

The first letter is Shin, which makes a consonant /sh/ sound. Having the stop Nikud sign, it is read as a consonant /sh/

The second letter is Mem, which makes a consonant /m/ sound. Having an /e/ Nikud sign, it is read as /me/

The third letter is Yod. Because the sound before the Yod is not /ee/, it can only be a consonant, read as /y/ (even though, here - it doesn't have the stop Nikud sign). Together with the second letter, the syllable is read as /mey/

The forth letter is Mem, making a consonant /m/ sound. Combined with the /ee/ Nikud sign, it is read as /mee/. The last letter is Yod which following an /ee/ sound and having no Nikud sign - tells us it is part of the /ee/ Nikud sign

WITH/WITHOUT NIKUD

Now that you learned about the /ee/ vowel sound, you know it can be represented by two different Nikud signs — one with the letter Yod and one without it. According to the Academy of the Hebrew Language, certain words with an /ee/ sound should include a Yod when written without Nikud but omit it when written with Nikud. Words like Mother, Bed, and Friday — which you just learned — are all examples of this rule.

Written with Nikud: אִמָּא שִׁשִׁי מִטָּה

Written without Nikud: אימא שישי מיטה

When a word falls under this rule, I'll show you both versions so you can get used to this as you expand your vocabulary.
When in doubt, write words with an /ee/ sound WITH a Yod letter.

TWO YOD LETTERS

If you see a word written without Nikud signs that has two Yod letters one next to each other, it's not a conspiracy to confuse you :) Typically, one Yod is part of the Nikud sign for the vowel sound /ee/, and the other is a consonant Yod.

Because the Nikud signs give us a better indication is the letter a consonant or a vowel, when these words are written with Nikud signs they usually have only one Yod letter.

	(ONE) SECOND	(HE) WILL GIVE	TEETH
Written With Nikud:	שְׁנִיָּה	יִתֵּן	שִׁנַּיִם
Written Without Nikud:	שנייה	ייתן	שיניים
	/sh-nee-'yah/	/yee-'ten/	/shee-'na-yeem/

/EE/ VOWEL SOUND: SUMMARY

The **/ee/** vowel sound is pronounced like the letters EE in the word Beep

/ee/ has two Nikud signs that are identical in sound. One has a Yod after it. When in doubt, write words with an /ee/ sound WITH a Yod letter.

Ḃ   Ḃי

/khee-'reek kha-'ser/   /khee-'reek ma-'le/

חִירִיק חָסֵר   חִירִיק מָלֵא

We remember them as the round beeping horn of a steering wheel

We draw them by making one dot under the letter, with or without a Yod letter right after

LET'S PRACTICE
The /ee/ Vowel Sound

ADD NIKUD SIGNS TO THE WORDS BELOW:

SONG	MAN	POT
שיר	איש	סיר
/sheer/	/eesh/	/seer/

CITY	CHAMELEON	BAG/PURSE
עיר	זקית	תיק
/eer/	/zee-'keet/	/teek/

If you have Hebrew 2 Workbook,
add Nikud to the words on pages 14, 24, 66.

Check how you did inside the free course.

GUESS WHAT? THE HARD PART'S OVER!

You're crushing it, and you're so close to the finish line! Just two more vowel sounds to go - and the best part? They're similar to the /ee/ sound you already know, so the hard part is behind you!

So let's dive in and tackle these last two vowel sounds together!
Once you're done, you'll have the entire Hebrew vowel system down like a champ!

Let's do this and conquer the final two sounds!

Lesson 10:

/0/
VOWEL SOUND

The
/o/
vowel sound is
pronounced
like
the letter O
in the word Or

The /o/ vowel sound in Hebrew
can be represented by two
different Nikud signs.

One includes the vowel Vav ו
letter as part of it, and the
other does not.

Let's start with the second
option.

THE FIRST NIKUD SIGN FOR THE /O/ VOWEL SOUND LOOKS LIKE THIS (X REPRESENTS THE LETTER)

This Nikud sign is above the letter between this and the next letter to it left

Draw it by making one clear dot at the top of the line in-between this letter and the next letter to its left.

1
•

EASILY REMEMBER THIS NIKUD SIGN AND THE SOUND IT MAKES

This Nikud sign

●

that looks like and is positioned as the dot in the question mark hovering ABOVE as we try to decide between 'this' OR 'that' represents the sound /o/ like in the word Or, located above the letter in-between it and the next letter.

The **/o/** vowel sound is pronounced like the letter O in the word Or

LET'S USE THIS NIKUD SIGN TO READ HEBREW WORDS:

Read about the dot inside the letter Dalet on p. 124

דֹב

A bear in Hebrew is /dov/

The first letter is Dalet. Dalet makes a consonant /d/ sound. Having an /o/ Nikud sign, it is read as /do/.

The last letter is Bet with no Dugesh, which makes a consonant /v/ sound. It has no Nikud sign, so we read it as a consonant, making a consonant /v/ sound.

CROWN YOURSELF WITH THIS:

רֹאשׁ

Head in Hebrew is /rosh/

The first letter is Resh. Resh makes a consonant /r/ sound. It has an /o/ Nikud sign, so we read it as /ro/.

The second letter is Alef. Having no Nikud sign indicates that it is a vowel Alef, which is silent.

The third letter is Shin. Shin makes a consonant /sh/ sound. Having no Nikud sign, we read it as a consonant, making a consonant /sh/ sound.

* A dot above the letter can only be an /o/ Nikud sign OR the dot that is part of the Shin/Sin letter (as you learned in Hebrew 1 and 2).

THE SECOND NIKUD SIGN FOR THE /O/ VOWEL SOUND LOOKS LIKE THIS (X REPRESENTS THE LETTER)

וֹX

This Nikud sign is above the letter Vav which comes after the letter assigned the /o/ sound.

Draw it by making one dot (identical to the first Nikud sign for /o/ you just learned) above the Vav letter that comes right after.

1

LET'S USE THIS NIKUD SIGN TO READ HEBREW WORDS:

אוֹר

Light in Hebrew is /or/

Because we have Nikud signs - like /o/ - that appear on the next letter (Vav), if a letter does not have a Nikud sign, we check the next letter to its left. If it is a Vav letter with a dot on top, that tells us the vowel sound of the letter before the Vav.

The first letter is Alef which can be a consonant or a vowel. Having no Nikud sign, we check the next letter. It is Vav with a dot on top, which tells us it is the Nikud sign for the Alef: We read the first letter /o/, and skip to the letter after the Vav.

The last letter is Resh which makes a consonant /r/ sound. Having no Nikud sign, We read it as a consonant, making a consonant /r/ sound.

BEEP BOOP BOP IN HEBREW:

רוֹבּוֹט

Robot in Hebrew is formally pronounced /ro-'bot/, and commonly /'ro-bot/

The first letter is Resh. Resh makes a consonant /r/ sound. It has no Nikud sign, and the next letter is a Vav with a dot on top, which tells us it is the Nikud sign for the Resh letter. We read the first letter /ro/, and skip to the letter after the Vav.

The third letter is Bet with a Dugesh. It makes a consonant /b/ sound. Having no Nikud sign, we check the next letter which is a Vav with a dot on top, and so we read the third letter /bo/, and skip to the letter after the Vav.

The last letter is Tet which makes a consonant /t/ sound. Having no Nikud sign, we read it as a consonant, making a consonant /t/ sound.

WHAT DO WE CALL THESE NIKUD SIGNS?

The names of the Nikud signs are not essential for reading using Nikud. If you want to know the names of the Nikud signs, here's that easy tip again: The first syllable of each Nikud sign name matches the vowel sound of the Nikud sign. This rule applies to all Nikud signs.

Let's see how it works with the two /o/ sound Nikud signs you just learned:

Ẋ   אׂX

חֹלָם חַסֵּר
This Nikud sign is called /kho-ˈlam kha-ˈser/

חֹלָם מָלֵא
This Nikud sign is called /kho-ˈlam ma-ˈle/

The first syllable in Kholam is /o/ just like the sound it represents. The second words in each name refer to whether it has a Vav or not: /ma-ˈle/ for Full = With a Vav, and /Kha-ˈser/ for Absent = Without a Vav.

WITH/WITHOUT NIKUD

Now that you learned about the /o/ vowel sound, you know it can be represented by two different Nikud signs — one with the letter Vav, and one without it. According to the Academy of the Hebrew Language, certain words with an /o/ sound should include a Vav when written without Nikud but omit it when written with Nikud. The Word Bear that you just learned is one example of this rule.

Written
With Nikud:

דֹּב

Written
Without Nikud:

דוֹב

Whenever a word falls under this rule, I'll show you both versions so you'll get used to it as you expand your vocabulary.
When in doubt, write words with an /o/ sound WITH a Vav letter.

/O/ VOWEL SOUND: SUMMARY

The
/o/
vowel sound is
pronounced
like
the letter O
in the word Or

/o/ has two Nikud signs that are basically the same. One has a Vav letter after it. When in doubt, write the /o/ sound WITH a Vav letter.

אֹ

/kho-'lam kha-'ser/

חוֹלָם חָסֵר

אוֹ

/ko-'lam ma-'le/

חוֹלָם מָלֵא

This sign that looks like and is positioned as the dot in a question mark hovering ABOVE as we try to decide between this OR that represents the sound /o/ as in the word Or.

We draw it by making one clear dot above the letter to its left, or above the Vav letter after it.

EXERCISES FOR MASTERY

ADD NIKUD SIGNS TO THE WORDS BELOW:

SOUND	GLASS / CUP	DRUM
קול	כוס	תף
/kol/	/kos/	/tof/
OX	QUE / LINE	MONKEY
שור	תור	קוף
/shor/	/tor/	/kof/

Check how you did inside the free course.

EXERCISES FOR MASTERY

WRITE THE WORDS BELOW IN ENGLISH USING THE PSP:

POLICE OFFICER	CLOCK / WATCH	POST / MAIL
 שׁוֹטֵר	 שָׁעוֹן	 דֹּאַר
/?/	/?/	/?/
COCOA DRINK	TENT	PLANE
 שׁוֹקוֹ	 אֹהֶל	 מָטוֹס
/?/	/?/	/?/

If you have Hebrew 1 Workbook,
add Nikud to the word on page 16.

Check how you did inside the free course.

Lesson 11:

/OO/
VOWEL SOUND

The
/oo/
vowel sound is
pronounced
like
the letters OO
in the word Oops

The /oo/ vowel sound in Hebrew can be represented by two different Nikud signs.

One includes the vowel Vav ו as part of it, and the other does not.

Let's start with the second option.

THE FIRST NIKUD SIGN FOR THE /OO/ VOWEL SOUND LOOKS LIKE THIS (X REPRESENTS THE LETTER)

This Nikud sign is under the letter.

Draw it by making three dots going down diagonally from left to right, starting with the top one.

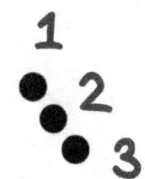

EASILY REMEMBER THIS NIKUD SIGN AND THE SOUND IT MAKES

This Nikud sign

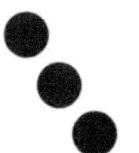

looks like 3 oranges falling from the tree

The
/oo/
vowel sound is pronounced like the letters OO in the word Oops

This Nikud sign that looks like 3 oranges falling from the tree makes an /oo/ sound like the /oo/ in the word Oops:
"Oops, 3 oranges just fell from the tree!"

LET'S USE THIS NIKUD SIGN TO READ HEBREW WORDS:

Read about the dot inside the letter Lamed on p. 124

סֻלָּם

A ladder in Hebrew is /soo-'lam/

Just like the ladder we climb on to pick oranges from the tree, only to see that 3 fell to the ground :)

The first letter is Samekh which makes a consonant /s/ sound. It has an /oo/ Nikud sign, and so we read it as /soo/.

The second letter is Lamed which makes a consonant /l/ sound. Having an /a/ Nikud sign, we read it as /la/.

The last letter is Mem (sofit). Mem makes a consonant /m/ sound. Having no Nikud sign and being at the end of the word, we read it as a consonant /m/.

BEARY CUTE WORD AHEAD:

Read about the dot inside the letter Dalet on p. 124

דֻּבִּי

A teddy bear in Hebrew is /'doo-bee/

The first letter is Dalet which makes a consonant /d/ sound. Having an /oo/ Nikud sign, we read it as /doo/.

The second letter is Bet with a Dagesh, making a consonant /b/ sound. Having an /ee/ Nikud sign, we read it as /bee/.

The last letter is Yod. Having no Nikud sign, and being a Yod letter after an /ee/ Nikud sign, that is our sign that it is a vowel Yod. It is part of this Nikud sign adding no sound to the existing /bee/ sound.

THE SECOND NIKUD SIGN FOR THE /OO/ VOWEL SOUND LOOKS LIKE THIS (X REPRESENTS THE LETTER)

·ΙX

This Nikud sign is attached to a Vav that follows the letter carrying the /oo/ sound. The dot is positioned mid-height to the left of the Vav letter.

Draw it by making one clear dot, and placing it mid-height to the left of the Vav letter that comes right after the letter.

1
●

EASILY REMEMBER THIS NIKUD SIGN AND THE SOUND IT MAKES

This Nikud sign

• |

Looks like the rounded OO's in Ooooops

The /oo/ vowel sound is pronounced like the letters OO in the word Oops

OOOOPS!

stretching all the way - like Oooops does - to the next (Vav) letter as a tiny O mid-height to the left of the Vav letter.

LET'S USE THIS NIKUD SIGN TO READ HEBREW WORDS:

סוּס

A horse in Hebrew is /soos/.

Since the /o/ and /oo/ Nikud signs can appear on the next letter (Vav), when a letter has no Nikud sign, we check if the next letter is a Vav with a dot on top or mid-height to its left. If it is, the preceding letter carries the /o/ or /oo/ sound (based on the position of the dot around the Vav letter).

The first letter is Samekh, which makes a consonant /s/ sound. Having no Nikud sign, we check the next letter. It is a Vav with a dot positioned mid-height to its left. That means, that the first letter is read as /soo/. We then skip the Vav, as it is part of the /oo/ Nikud sign.

The last letter is Samekh which makes a consonant /s/ sound. Having no Nikud sign at the end of a word, we read it as a consonant /s/.

TIME FOR A SWEET WORD:

עוּגָה

A cake in Hebrew is /oo-'gah/

The first letter is Ayin. Ayin can make each of the 5 vowel sounds in Hebrew based on its Nikud sign. In this case, it has no Nikud sign, and the next letter is Vav with a dot mid-height to its left, so we read the Ayin as /oo/, and skip to the letter after the Vav (as it is part of the Nikud sign).

The third letter is Gimel which makes a consonant /g/ sound. Having an /a/ Nikud sign, we read it as /ga/.

The last letter is He. He can be a consonant or a vowel. Having no Nikud sign means it is a vowel. A vowel He at the end of a word is silent with more air flow than vowel Alef or Ayin = The sound of the last syllable is /gah/.

WHAT DO WE CALL THESE NIKUD SIGNS?

You already know that knowing the names of the Nikud names is not needed for reading and writing with Nikud.
You also know that the vowel sound each Nikud sign makes is identical to the first syllable of that Nikud sign name.

Let's see how it works with the two /oo/ sound Nikud signs you just learned:

X
.:

·וX

קֻבּוּץ

This Nikud sign is called /koo-'boots/

שׁוּרוּק

This Nikud sign is called /shoo-'rook/

The first syllable in /shoo-'rook/ and /koo-'boots/ is /oo/
just like the sound they represent.

WITH/WITHOUT NIKUD

Now that you learned about the /oo/ vowel sound, you know it can be represented by two different Nikud signs — one with the letter Vav, and one without it. According to the Academy of the Hebrew Language, certain words with an /oo/ sound should include a Vav when written without Nikud but omit it when written with Nikud. The Words Teddy bear and Ladder you just learned are examples of this rule.

Written
With Nikud: סֻלָּם   דֻּבִּי

Written
Without Nikud: סולם   דובי

whenever a word falls under this rule, I'll show you both versions so you can become familiar with this as you expand your vocabulary. When in doubt, write words with an /oo/ sound WITH a Vav letter.

/OO/ VOWEL SOUND: SUMMARY

The
/oo/
vowel sound is
pronounced
like
the letters OO
in the word Oops

/oo/ has two Nikud signs that are basically the same. One has a Vav after it. When in doubt, write words with an /oo/ sound WITH a Vav letter:

קֻ

שׁוּרֻק

/koo-'boots/

קֻבֻּץ

/shoo-'rook/

שׁוּרֻק

OOOOPS!

We remember them as Oops: 3 round apples fell from the tree, just like in Ooops, or one that stretched all the way to the next Vav letter

We draw them by making either 3 diagonal dots under the letter, or one dot mid-height to the left of the Vav letter that comes after the letter

PERFECT YOUR CRAFT: PRACTICE EXERCISES

ADD NIKUD SIGNS TO THE WORDS BELOW:

PAIR/COUPLE	PARROT	DOLL
זוג	תכּי	בּבּה
/zoog/	/'too-kee/	/boo-'bah/

KETTLE	BROWN	TABLE
קמקום	חום	שלחן
/koom-'koom/	/khoom/	/shool-'khan/

Check how you did inside the free course.

PERFECT YOUR CRAFT: PRACTICE EXERCISES

ADD NIKUD SIGNS TO THE WORDS BELOW:

SOUND	BALL	SHIRT
קול	כדור	חלצה
/Kol/	/ka-'door/	/khool-'tsah/

STRAWBERRY	CAT	SUGAR
תות	חתול	סכר
/toot/	/kha-'tool/	/soo-'kar/

If you have Hebrew 1 Workbook, add Nikud to the words on pages 24, 46, 54, 60, 78, 80.

If you have Hebrew 2 Workbook, add Nikud to the words on pages 36, 50, 54, 76, 84.

Check how you did inside the free course.

ELITE LEVEL PRACTICE

READ THE WORDS BELOW, AND WRITE THEM IN ENGLISH LETTERS USING THE PSP:

BAD / EVIL (Adjective)	FRIEND	EVIL (Noun)
רַע	רֵעַ	רֹעַ
/?/	/?/	/?/

Check how you did inside the free course.

Lesson 12:

LESS COMMON & EXTRA NIKUD SIGNS

DOTS INSIDE THE LETTERS

When reading Hebrew written with Nikud, you'll notice dots inside various letters.

In Hebrew 1 & 2, you learned all about the Dagesh — which letters it appears in, when (and how) it changes the sound, and when it doesn't.

The other case of dots inside letters are there to indicate a slightly more stressed sound.

Since in this case, there's no noticeable difference in pronunciation with or without these dots — and most native Hebrew speakers wouldn't know how to use them — you can safely ignore them while writing (and reading) using Nikud.

UNCOMMON NIKUD SIGNS

When reading the Bible and other Hebrew texts with Nikud, you may come across three uncommon Nikud signs that indicate a shortened vowel sound. Since they don't create a noticeable difference in pronunciation — and most Hebrew speakers wouldn't know how to use them — all you need to know is how to read them in case you come across them in your reading. You can safely skip them when writing using Nikud.

As can see below, they appear as the vowel signs that you learned with an extra : sign to their right.

/a/ sound	/a/ sound	/e/ sound
X	X	X
ֲ	ֳ	ֱ
/kha-ˈtaf pa-ˈtakh/	/kha-ˈtaf ka-ˈmats/	/kha-ˈtaf se-ˈgol/
חֲטָף פָּתַח	חֲטָף קָמָץ	חֲטָף סֶגּוֹל

EXCEPTION: "STOLEN" /A/

As you learned, when we see a Nikud sign, we add the vowel sound of that Nikud sign to the consonant sound of that letter, for example - /kha/ if the Nikud sign is an /a/, and the letter is Khet.

One uncommon exception I want you to know is this:

When the last letter of a word is Khet (ח), Ayin (ע), or He (ה) AND it has a Patakh (/a/ Nikud sign) AND the vowel sound before the last letter is /e/, /ee/, /o/, or /oo/ — the /a/ sound of the Nikud sign is added BEFORE the consonant sound, creating an /akh/ syllable in the same example instead of /kha/. This phenomenon is called "stolen Patakh" in Hebrew, and it looks like this:

Wind

רוּחַ

/'roo-akh/

Apple

תַפּוּחַ

/ta-'poo-akh/

YOU DID IT! WHAT'S NEXT?

You've completed all your Hebrew reading and writing skills 🎉
But your journey doesn't end here. Here are the perfect next steps to keep your progress going:

1 **Keep Practicing & Expanding** — Use my free daily and weekly Hebrew lessons to continue building on everything you learned in Hebrew 1, 2, and 3. Make sure you:
- Subscribe to my YouTube channel (Hebrew by Inbal) and click the notification bell for lessons exclusive to YouTube.
- Follow Hebrew by Inbal on your preferred social media platform for daily free lessons.
- Check your inbox every Sunday at noon (ET) for my weekly Hebrew email lesson.

2 **Stay Updated on New Hebrew Readers** — If you haven't already, join the free Hebrew 3 course to practice, check your work, and get updates on my new books and readers coming very soon!

3 **Reinforce Your Learning with Cursive** — Strengthen your retention by rewriting all your newfound words in cursive script. This practice will boost your handwriting, reading fluency, and Nikud skills.

4 **Ready to Speak & Understand Hebrew?** Reading is just the beginning — now let's get you speaking like a local! Join me in my Practically Speaking Hebrew online program and gain the clarity and confidence to have real-life Hebrew conversations: **learn.hebrewbyinbal.com**

Thank you for letting me be part of your Hebrew journey! Your progress has been incredible, and I'm so proud of how far you've come. I'm here to support you as you continue to grow and excel.

Your proud teacher,

Inbal Amit